I AM HEALING

A Child's Guide to Resilience

Written and illustrated by GAYLE GURCHIEK

Sky Pony Press
New York

To my beloved son.

This book is for you—my heart, my hope, and my strength.

As I journey through healing, you remind me every day of the power of love, courage, and resilience.

May you always know that you are my greatest gift, and through every word in this book, I carry you with me, always.

With all my love,

Mom

I would like to express my heartfelt gratitude to the following wonderful people who helped make this book a reality.

A special thanks to Matthew Schipper for his incredible talents in photographing the artwork, capturing each piece with such care and precision.

And to my daddy, your love, guidance, and endless support have been the foundation of everything I do. Thank you for always believing in me.

Thank you all for being a part of this adventure!

I am like the jellyfish, floating gently in the sea. I move through challenges with ease, wrapping my soft arms around myself. Each tender movement is a reminder:

I am loved.

I am like the snail, moving slowly but with purpose. Sometimes, I feel like things are taking too long. But I know, like the snail, that each moment brings me closer to healing.

I am patient.

I am like the macaw, full of vibrant colors and hope. When my heart feels heavy, I take a deep breath and imagine myself healing. Just like the macaw, soaring on bright wings through the sky, my hope rises.

I am improving.

I am like the loon, gliding gracefully across still waters. When my mind is full of worry, I find balance in quiet moments. I know that sometimes stillness helps me heal, just like the calm waters that soothe the loon.

I am peaceful.

I am like the fox, curious and full of wonder. Even in the toughest times, I look for beauty and magic in the world. Like the fox, I keep exploring, always finding something that makes me smile.

I am resourceful.

I am like the elephant, gentle and kind. I share love and empathy with those around me. Love helps heal all things.

I am compassionate.

I am like the hummingbird, small but mighty. I sip the nectar of life, knowing even the tiniest actions give me strength. Sometimes, the smallest steps lead to the greatest healing.

I am strong.

I am like the whale, happy and free. Out of my element, I rise above and see the world from a new perspective. I know that healing can happen, and the world is full of possibilities.

I am boundless.

I am like the frog, hopping through the bamboo forest. When I'm unsure of myself, my friend the elephant shows me that strength comes from within. With each leap, I feel more empowered to face whatever comes my way.

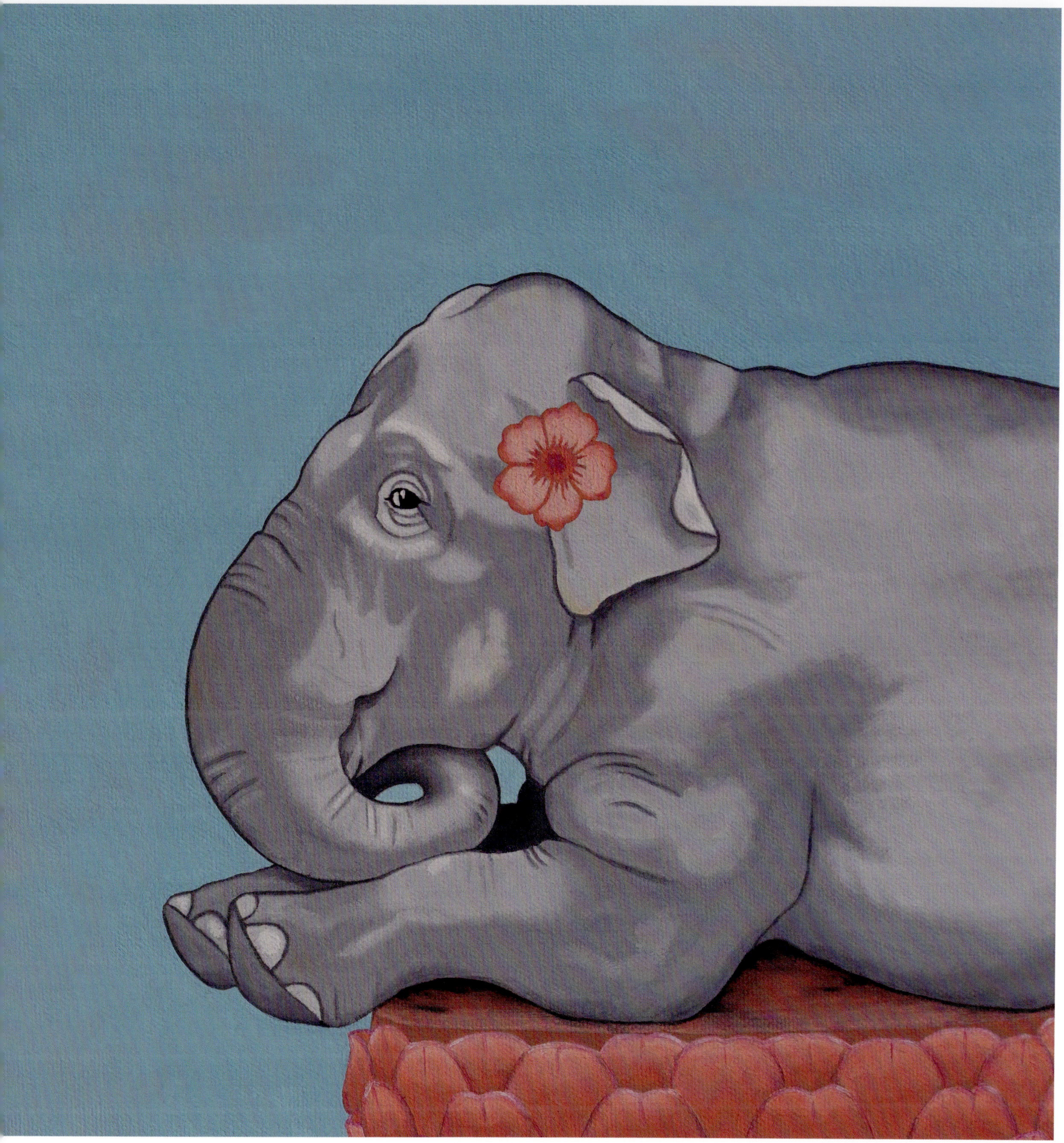

I am resilient.

I am like the lion, brave and bold. I stand tall and roar with courage in the face of fear. Even on days when I feel afraid, I remember the lion inside me, and I know I will carry on.

I am courageous.

I am like the squirrel, playful and full of energy. I find joy in nature. With every step, every laugh, and every discovery, my spirit heals.

I am joyful.

I am like the owl, knowledgeable and thoughtful. I listen to my heart and trust in its intuition. With every positive thought, I find courage.

I am wise.

I am like the butterfly, light and graceful. I spread hope wherever I go. With every flutter of my wings, I dream that healing is possible.

I am brilliant.

I am like the chimpanzee, adventurous and curious. With my friends beside me, I know I am never alone. We laugh, explore, and face each day, knowing that we are better together.

I am strong.

I am like the seahorse, steady and resilient. When the waters are rough, I hold on tight. No matter what comes, I never give up.

I am determined.

I am like the bunny, hopping through the fields. I know that healing is something we do together. With kindness, love, and patience, we create a brighter world.

I am hopeful.

When the world feels big and the road ahead seems long, I am strong. I am learning to heal, one moment, one breath, one step at a time. I am a warrior. I am whole. I am light. I will shine brighter and share my love with the world.

I am healthy.

Sky Pony Press books may be purchased in bulk at special discounts for sales promotion, corporate gifts, fund-raising, or educational purposes. Special editions can also be created to specifications. For details, contact the Special Sales Department, Sky Pony Press, 307 West 36th Street, 11th Floor, New York, NY 10018 or info@skyhorsepublishing.com.

Visit our website at www.skyponypress.com.

10 9 8 7 6 5 4 3 2 1

Manufactured in China, 2025
This product conforms to CPSIA 2008

Library of Congress Control Number: 2025935243

Cover design by Kai Texel
Cover illustration by Gayle Gurchiek

Print ISBN: 978-1-5107-8493-2
Ebook ISBN: 978-1-5107-8494-9

RESOURCES

- The National Children's Cancer Society (NCCS): https://thenccs.org/helpful-resources/
- Sunrise Day Camp: The world's only dedicated day camps for children with cancer and their siblings, all offered free of charge. https://sunrisedaycamp.org
- Alex's Lemonade Stand: A foundation for childhood cancer. https://www.alexslemonade.org/childhood-cancer/for-families
- First Descents: Provides life-changing outdoor adventures for young adults impacted by cancer and MS. https://firstdescents.org/